ISBN 0-7683-2049-6
D.L.TO: 459-1998
Text by Flavia and Lisa Weedn
Illustrations by Flavia Weedn
© Weedn Family Trust
www.flavia.com

Published in 1998 by Cedco Publishing Company
100 Pelican Way, San Rafael, California 94901
For a free catalog of other Cedco® products, please write
to the address above, or visit our website: www.cedco.com

Printed in Spain

The artwork for each picture is digitally mastered using acrylic on canvas.

A WOMAN'S PERSONAL JOURNEY

Passages

Flavia and Lisa Weedn
Illustrated by Flavia Weedn

Cedco Publishing Company • San Rafael, California

As impassioned women, we strive to
create **beauty,** hope, and abundance
in our lives and for our loved ones.
We take on many roles as caretakers
and *nurturers*, professionals
and homemakers, mothers and daughters,
sisters and wives.
The theater of life asks us to be strong and
radiant, loving and resilient,
tender and *graceful* and wise.
Indeed, we are all these things and more, for
within each of us is a **remarkable** being.
When life's path brings changes or challenges,
we are forced to stop and *listen* to our deepest voice within.
And the traits we sometimes hide are often
our greatest STRENGTHS: our vulnerabilities,
our simplicities and complexities,
our yearning to *dance* to the
music of our dreams.

If we give ourselves permission to feel

the spectrum of the WOMEN we are,

and to honestly listen to the

WISDOM of our HEARTS,

we discover courage we never knew we had—

a kind of beauty that can give us back the person

we may have thought was lost.

This journal is designed to help you

celebrate the woman you've become. Leading you

forward on a path of discovery and healing,

you will be encouraged to listen to your most private

thoughts, to uncover renewed hopes

and re-awakened dreams.

It is our hope that as you venture

through the stages of your life,

you will hear the echo of joy and triumph, and

embrace the exquisite gift it is

to be you.

Flavia

Table of Contents

Dress Rehearsal

The Theater of Life

In Time to the Music

Dress Rehearsal

*B*efore I can UNDERSTAND where I'm

going, it is important for me to

understand *where I've been.*

The roots of my heart, the voices of my past

are all a part of the **woman** I am today.

As I touch upon old scripts, let me

remember how far I've come;

and let me always hold **sacred** each

shimmering thread

that makes up the

exquisite fabric of *me.*

Looking Back

The Girl I Was

Echoes of My Mother

Echoes of My Father

Thank you for the yesterdays my heart
still holds in its pockets.

Early Scripts

Weaving Patterns

Finding Peace

Heroes and Mentors

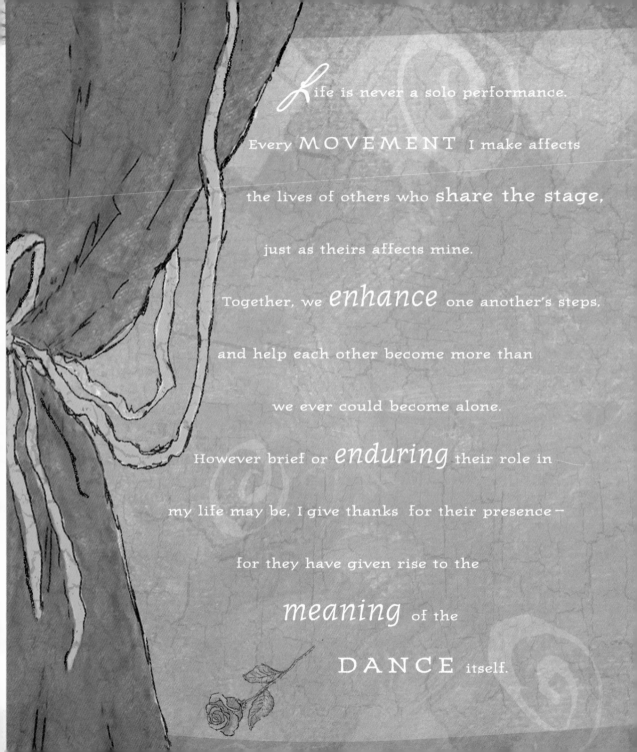

Life is never a solo performance.

Every MOVEMENT I make affects

the lives of others who share the stage,

just as theirs affects mine.

Together, we enhance one another's steps,

and help each other become more than

we ever could become alone.

However brief or enduring their role in

my life may be, I give thanks for their presence—

for they have given rise to the

meaning of the

DANCE itself.

The Theater of Life

Scenes Begun

Who's on Stage

Hands I Hold

Sometimes there is someone who takes time
enough to listen—someone who cares about us
when we lose, and who loves us even when we're wrong.

Friends and Family

Encouraging Words

Unspoken Lines

Pursuing Career

Yearning to Dance

In Motion

The Next Scene

Every

moment

in time

holds a

wondrous

gift

in its

hands.

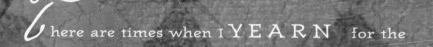

$\mathcal{T}$here are times when I YEARN for the

uncomplicatedness of my youth, back when time was simple and life

was a single ballet. Other times I revel in the WONDER of my

multiplicity. My capacity to love, the strength of my hands, and

the courage of my believing heart reminds me that

life is not meant to be a recital, but a

grand performance.

This is when I know I have

grown and that I am a

remarkable me—

for I am the author,

the composer, the orchestra

and the swan.

In Time to the Music

The Roles I Play

The Dance of Time

The Woman

The Lover

Nothing is more necessar___ ___ the heart
than to love and b___ ___ ___ ___ ___rn.

The Mother

The Daughter

At Work

Art Play

Private Time

Just For Me

Take time to nurture yourself, for in doing so, you will have more to give to others.

Entrances & Exits

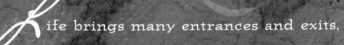

Life brings many entrances and exits,

some as WELCOME as a

soothing wind, others filled with heartache.

But life is change, and each new beginning

is a PASSAGE IN TIME bringing

with it refined meanings and new perspectives to

the woman I am. Every change is an opportunity

and a blessing; every moment a new me

is being born. Greater happiness

and WONDROUS SURPRISES await,

if only I have the courage to

walk through the door.

When I finally LISTEN

to the wisdom of my heart,

I begin to understand that time

never takes the precious things away.

All the BEAUTY and substance of me,

which I mistakenly thought were lost, are right here

within my reach—threads to every memory,

silver cords woven into every new day.

Let me always remember that time is not a thief.

It is a friend, a *healer*, and a

maker of dreams.

The Voice of My Heart

$\mathcal{S}$tepping out of the shadows and into the light

can be both exhilarating and frightening.

But I have learned that to live fully, I must be

unafraid to E M B R A C E all that living brings.

I now celebrate the beauty of my heart

and find **peace** in knowing that I don't have

to be everything, just me.

The most sacred gifts I own are the

passion of my dreams and the

courage to B E L I E V E   I N   M Y S E L F.

With this knowledge I am becoming the

champion of my soul—

for my spirit, my beloved spirit, is

learning how

to D A N C E.

Stepping Into the Light

With Grace and Gratitude

Other Flavia Books for Adults:

Heart and Soul
A Personal Tale of Love and Romance

Heaven and Earth
A Journal of Dreams and Awakenings

Dear Little One
A Memory Journal of Baby's First Year

Kindred Spirits
An Illustrated Address Book

Celebrations of Life
A Birthday and Anniversary Book

Flavia Books for Children:

The Little Snow Bear

The Enchanted Tree

The Elephant Prince

The Star Gift

Photo by Claudia Kunin

Flavia Weedn is one of America's leading contemporary inspirational writers and illustrators. Her work has touched the lives of millions for over three decades. Offering a kind of hope for the human spirit, Flavia portrays the basic excitement, simplicity and beauty she sees in the ordinary things of life. Lisa Weedn, Flavia's daughter and co-author, shares her mother's philosophy and passion. Their collaborative writings celebrate life and embrace meaningful core values. It is their wish to shine a beacon of hope into the lives of others by encouraging the belief that we all have a significant contribution to make in this lifetime and every dream can be realized. Their work includes numerous books, collections of fine stationery goods, giftware, and lifestyle products distributed worldwide. Flavia and Lisa live in Santa Barbara, California.